72

D065669

THE
BIRDWATCHER'S
LOGBOOK

First published in 2003 by New Holland Publishers (UK) Ltd
London • Cape Town • Sydney • Auckland

Garfield House, 86–88 Edgware Road, London W2 2EA, United Kingdom
www.newhollandpublishers.com

80 Mckenzie Street, Cape Town 8001, South Africa

Level 1/Unit 4, 14 Aquatic Drive, Frenchs Forest, NSW 2086, Australia

218 Lake Road, Northcote, Auckland, New Zealand

1 3 5 7 9 10 8 6 4 2

Copyright © 2003 in text Dominic Couzens
Copyright © 2003 in artworks New Holland Publishers (UK) Ltd
Copyright © 2003 New Holland Publishers (UK) Ltd

All rights reserved. No part of this publication may be reproduced, stored in any retrieval system or transmitted, in any
form or by any means, electronic, mechanical, photocopying, recording or otherwise, without the prior written
permission of the publishers and copyright holders.

ISBN 1 84330 150 4

Publishing Manager: Jo Hemmings
Project Editor: Camilla MacWhannell
Cover Design: Alan Marshall
Design: Alan Marshall & Gulen Shevki
Production: Joan Woodroffe

Reproduction by Pica Digital Pte Ltd, Singapore
Printed and bound by Kyodo Printing Co (Singapore) Pte Ltd

Artwork Acknowledgements
Artworks including cover by David Daly

Additional Artworks
Stephen Message: p162; p163 (Shag); p166 (Oystercatcher, Avocet, Little Ringed Plover, Ringed Plover, Dotterel,
Golden Plover, Grey Plover, Lapwing, Knot, Sanderling, Little Stint, Temminck's Stint, Curlew Sandpiper, Purple
Sandpiper, Dunlin, Ruff); p167 (Jack Snipe, Snipe, Woodcock, Black-tailed Godwit, Whimbrel, Curlew, Spotted
Redshank, Redshank, Greenshank, Green Sandpiper, Wood Sandpiper, Common Sandpiper, Turnstone, Pomarine Skua,
Arctic Skua, Great Skua); p168 (Sandwich Tern, Roseate Tern, Common Tern, Arctic Tern, Little Tern, Black Tern,
Guillemot, Razorbill, Black Guillemot, Little Auk, Puffin).

Clive Byers: p164 (Red Kite, Marsh Harrier); p165 (Hen Harrier, Montagu's Harrier, Merlin, Hobby, Red Grouse, Black
Grouse, Grey Partridge, Quail).

THE BIRDWATCHER'S LOGBOOK

A Record of Your Birding Year

DOMINIC COUZENS

NEW HOLLAND

CONTENTS

Chaffinches

Pheasant feeding

INTRODUCTION

Swallows

HOW TO USE THIS BOOK

Although *The Birdwatcher's Logbook* carries an introduction, and has an illustrated check list at the back, it is essentially authored and illustrated by you. The heart of the book is designed to be filled with your own notes, sketches, lists and comments. After each birdwatching trip, fill it in back at home, and it will form a record of your birdwatching year, whether in the garden, your favourite patch, or on your travels around the country. On the pages of this logbook you can store your ornithological history, its successes and failures, revelations and travails.

I have included advice, especially for the beginner, on how to make notes and why, plus information on learning to watch and identify birds. There is a section on what is going on during the four seasons of the year, and suggestions are dotted throughout the diary on what to look for, where to go and what to do at certain times. There is a species tick list at the back, in which you can register your records, and an illustrated check list to help you identify a number of the species that you are most likely to encounter.

But, of course, you don't have to use any of it. Now you've got it, this is your book. May your notes and pictures enliven these pages, and make *The Birdwatcher's Logbook* a special reminder of your very own bird-watching year.

MAKING NOTES

What's the difference between a good bird-watcher and an outstanding birdwatcher? And what's the difference between a beginner who struggles and a beginner who improves quickly? The answer is the same in both cases: the fast-track birder takes notes.

But why must everyone's birds end up on paper? Aren't there lots of excellent bird books showing every possible way to identify a species and describing every possible detail of its life? Hasn't it all been written down before? Do I really have to add to this mass of information? No, you don't, but you will be missing out. There are several reasons why note-taking is so necessary.

Notes, for one thing, crystallize facts by dragging them from head-knowledge into the realm of experience. You might read in a book that a Fieldfare has a grey head, but that is not the same as assenting to it in your notes for the day. In this way, facts will become easier to remember.

Note-taking will also teach you how to observe birds. Writing things down will make you methodical in your observation and increase your eye for detail. Since every person is different and, in the same way, every individual bird is also slightly different, these details count. It is not too far-fetched to say that your notes are unique. However inexperienced you are, you are quite likely to stumble across a very singular interpretation of song, behaviour or plumage that could be helpful to other birdwatchers.

Many people ask, 'What sort of notes should I make?' Apart from recording the basics such as what birds were seen and when, how many of which sex or age were seen, where they were and what the weather conditions were like, the content of your notes is a matter for your own experience and personal taste. As suggested above, recording plumage details of selected species in word and sketch will make you a better observer. Recording behaviour traits will make you appreciate the complexities of what you are watching. And recording subjective details, such as the aesthetics, the company you kept and how you felt at the time, will make for a more entertaining read later on. It's up to you.

Of course, the greatest value gained from your notes will be their role in documenting your memories: what you have seen, what you have heard, and what you have learnt. So perhaps the most important question to ask, when deciding what to write down, will be: 'What will I want to remember?'

USING THE SPECIES TICK LIST

The tick list on page 158 can be used as a summary of birds seen month-by-month throughout the year. It's included for those who enjoy adding up their totals of species, both for each month, and for the year as a whole. Space is left to tick the respective column when the bird has been seen.

For beginners, and for those who prefer to stay local, 120-150 species is a respectable total for a year's birdwatching. For somebody who actively watches birds throughout the year, and is prepared to travel a little, a total of about 200 species would equally be a good 'score', and 100 would be good for a month's work. If one is prepared to use information phone lines and pagers, and then follow their directions to various corners of the country where rare birds have been found, the total can fairly soar. This logbook, and its list including regular species, is not designed to be used by such list-oriented 'twitchers'.

Science and tradition dictate that birds are always listed in a certain sequence. This sequence begins with the birds that are considered to be most primitive, having their origins early in the fossil record, and ends

with the most 'advanced' birds, those that are thought to have developed later along the rambling path of evolutionary progress.

It's a sensible way to list them, and carries the advantage of always grouping related species close together, but there is a snag to this system of listing in that it is difficult to follow. If, for example, you wish to tick off your Yellowhammer sighting for July, there's no easy way to find Yellowhammer except to look down the list and simply learn the sequence. Birds that live in the same habitat, such as seabirds, are not necessarily listed together, and neither are some birds that look similar but are not closely related, such as Swift and Swallow. Therefore, the sequence is not borne of convenience, but is an elegant representation of how complex birds really are.

GOING BIRDWATCHING

To go birdwatching, all you really have to do is go for a walk and use your eyes. Or you could watch the birds in your garden, if you have one. One of the delights of the hobby is that birds are abundant, ubiquitous, and free of charge.

It won't be long, however, before you will want to know what the names of the birds are, and for that you need an identification book or, as birdwatchers call it, a 'Field Guide'. A garden bird book is often an excellent start (see Recommended Reading on page 174), and then, if your hobby expands, you'll need a book with broader geographical coverage. There are dozens of different field guides, but here are a few suggestions: buy one with paintings, not with photographs; buy one that has at least three illustrations per bird; buy one without too many species; and buy one which has a decent amount of explanatory text.

Almost immediately, you'll also find you need a pair of binoculars, which constitutes the first major expense for a birdwatcher. Nowadays, there are a large number of models on the market, mostly very good, but it pays to be discerning. Avoid the high street;

instead, get your pair from a nature reserve, from the RSPB, or from one of the specialist stockists (*see* page 175). Such providers understand the needs of birdwatchers.

When you're buying binoculars, take your time. Try various different models. Explain that you're a beginner, and ask for advice. Don't be beguiled by models with large magnification, a figure in the range from x8 to x10 is usually sufficient. There are two specifications given on binoculars, such as 10x50; the first is the magnification, the second is the diameter of the objective lens in millimetres. The latter gives an indication of the brightness of the expected image, and a figure at least four times that of the magnification is required.

Once you are in the right place, test various models for weight and comfort as well as clarity and brightness. However good your binoculars are, they must be suitable for you. Prices obviously vary, but you should be able to pick up a reasonable pair for £150–£200.

Armed with binoculars, a notebook and a field guide, you now need some appropriate outdoor clothing. Remember, you're dressing to watch birds, not to look good in the high street. Birdwatching involves quite a bit of standing around, so you must wrap up warm. Your clothes should be comfortable, soberly coloured (not bright red or yellow), and not too noisy. Rustles and squeaks will disturb the birds. Needless to say, in this country your clothes should also be waterproof, and that includes headgear. Umbrellas are not appropriate for birdwatching; they scare birds away and make it difficult to hold binoculars. Birdwatching sites are often wet and muddy, so get yourself a good pair of walking boots.

You're now fully geared up, so all that remains is to go and watch the birds. Move around quietly, avoid rapid movements, and keep your first expeditions local, so that you can get to know your common birds first.

Very soon, you'll be looking for good places to watch birds, and you'll also want advice and guidance from other birdwatchers. This is where The Wildlife Trusts can help you. They have a large network of nature reserves and local members' groups which can be contacted through head office (*see* Useful Addresses on page 175).

IDENTIFYING BIRDS

A good birdwatcher sees an unfamiliar bird and doesn't jump to conclusions, preferring instead to observe as much detail as possible, and then work from the detail to the identification. Most of us are fairly lazy, and try to short cut this approach. We see a bird, remember a few cursory features, then fit our memory to a picture in a book. The problem is, this method is not methodical enough; it leaves too many gaps. We will end up with too many descriptions that read 'it was brown with red legs,' when, had we, for example, recorded the shape of the bill, we might have been able to come up with the correct name.

Identifying birds is all about looking for the right plumage features and the right aspects of shape, size, voice and behaviour. All these must, if possible, be taken in while the bird is being watched, which is often not a very long time. The secret of good birdwatching is using this time to accumulate all the necessary clues. In short, when we are watching, we must really look.

Learning the names given to the parts of a bird is essential, because it will help us to form quick descriptions in our mind: 'crown streaked, black eye-stripe, green nape...' It will also help us to verify our descriptions in the bird books. Although a much neglected part of birdwatching, knowing these technical terms actually makes life easier.

Apart from plumage, there are many other important aspects to look for and consider when identifying birds. What, for example, is the shape of the bird, including its bill (the bill is often critical in a diagnosis, especially of a wader), tail, wings and legs? What habitat is it in, and what is the season? Is it making any sounds? What sort of behaviour is it exhibiting?

Birdwatchers often use the jargon word 'jizz' to describe that hard-to-define combination of shape and behaviour that makes the light go on under the name of a certain bird when it is seen. For example, the way a mouse-like Treecreeper shuffles up a trunk soon becomes an easier clue to its identity than its colour combination of brown and white. As a birdwatcher becomes more experienced, these clues become more and more important. But beware – a jizz diagnosis cuts across the methodical approach to birdwatching, and has many pitfalls.

Many birders completely ignore the fact that birds make sounds. This is a pity, because the voices of birds are often the very best clue to their identity. True, it is difficult to learn them. But consider this – how many human voices can you recognize? Dozens – definitely; hundreds – probably. Don't give up on bird sounds too soon.

Here are a few hints for learning bird sound. First of all, begin your efforts in winter, when only a few species are singing. Then get into the habit of listening and describing what a sound is like. Is it fast or slow? Is it angry? Is it repeated? How many different notes are there? Does the sound remind you of anything, such as a cough, splutter or hiccup? Can you put the sound into words, such as 'pitchou' or 'chissick' (Marsh Tit and Pied Wagtail respectively)? If you're on your own, you might like to say the sound back to yourself, or try to imitate it. Once you've got into these good habits on your own, find a friendly, patient expert to help you. And lastly, don't try too hard; if you learn half a dozen bird songs or calls a season, you are doing very well indeed.

PARTS OF A BIRD

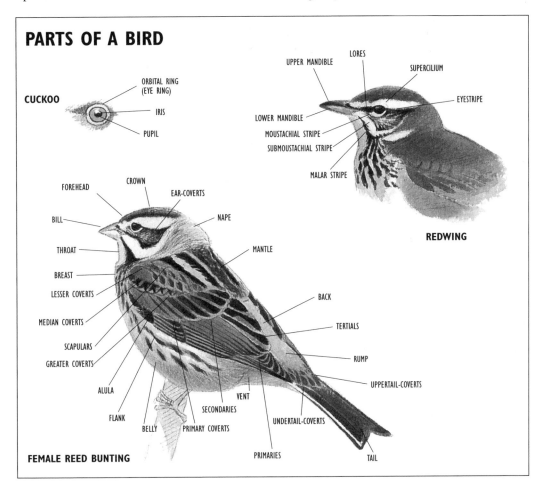

CUCKOO

ORBITAL RING (EYE RING)
IRIS
PUPIL

UPPER MANDIBLE
LORES
SUPERCILIUM
EYESTRIPE
LOWER MANDIBLE
MOUSTACHIAL STRIPE
SUBMOUSTACHIAL STRIPE
MALAR STRIPE

REDWING

FOREHEAD
CROWN
EAR-COVERTS
BILL
NAPE
THROAT
MANTLE
BREAST
LESSER COVERTS
MEDIAN COVERTS
BACK
SCAPULARS
TERTIALS
GREATER COVERTS
RUMP
ALULA
UPPERTAIL-COVERTS
VENT
FLANK
SECONDARIES
BELLY
PRIMARY COVERTS
UNDERTAIL-COVERTS
PRIMARIES
TAIL

FEMALE REED BUNTING

BIRDWATCHING IN WINTER

DECEMBER TO FEBRUARY

Most people think that winter is the time to stay indoors. But, for birdwatchers, winter means big flocks, spectacular movements, action-packed gardens, and birds in crisp, clean plumage. It's a time to appreciate and savour.

The leaf fall of autumn is like curtain up, revealing scenes that are hidden for much of the rest of the year. Birds like Treecreepers and woodpeckers suddenly become easier to find in winter, and the feather colours of under-appreciated species, such as Blue Tits and Chaffinches shine in sharp relief against the tired hues of leafless branches. Woodland, in particular, becomes an easier place in which to watch birds.

The garden buzzes with bird activity, especially when sharp frosts or snowfalls set in, or when the wild stock of food begins to run out in the woods and fields in January and February. Bird feeding stations attract a stream of visitors.

Although most people think that their garden is home to just a few Blue or Great Tits, the reality is that each garden will attract at least 100 different individuals of each species a week. These hungry birds in turn attract predators such as Sparrowhawks, and over the winter the hunter and hunted play out their grim drama in many a genteel setting amidst comfortable suburbia.

Winter is also a time when birds everywhere tend to gather in flocks, partly for safety, and partly because more eyes spy more food. The winter scene is full of swirling groups of birds, many of them eye-catching. Farmland holds flocks of finches and lapwings, woodland plays host to roaming flocks of tits, estuaries teem with waders, and ponds and marshes attract ducks and geese. Lots of birds make lots of noise, giving many of winter's best memories a massed soundtrack of wild voices.

These winter hordes are often not British birds, but visitors from north and east Europe. When we think of migration, most of us envisage a Swallow or Cuckoo making a treacherous journey to the forgiving climate of Africa for the winter. We forget that, as far as the rest of Europe is concerned, we have a mild, ice-free climate, and to an Arctic bird we are the equivalent of Africa. Just as many birds use us as a winter refuge as depart in the autumn. The obvious arrivals are our traditional visitors such as Redwings and Fieldfares, Bramblings and Waxwings, northern swans and geese. But visiting in even greater numbers are the 'hidden migrants',

Waxwing

foreign nationals of familiar species such as Blackbirds, Goldcrests, Tufted Ducks, Black-headed Gulls and Chaffinches. They are welcome invaders and give every corner of the country an international feel.

There is no better way to spend a winter day than to visit a tidal estuary. The birds that come here include large numbers of true Arctic dwellers, which breed on the tundra at daring latitudes. A good estuary will teem with waders and ducks, and if you manage to time your visit to a couple of hours before or after high tide, you should witness some dramatic comings and goings. For in an estuary the tide determines the timetable. At high tide the productive mud is covered, and everybody rests; but as soon as the water ebbs, rich feeding areas open up and the birds will hasten there, flying together in excited flocks. A rising or ebbing tide is like a school bell, summoning everyone to their places.

Estuaries are like refectories, providing food simultaneously for huge numbers of birds, each with slightly different tastes and methods of feeding. Curlews probe their long bills carefully into the mud for worms, shorter-billed Dunlins scamper and pick for tiny crustaceans and snails, Grey Plovers stand still and watch over the surface before running and grabbing a morsel, such as a crab, on the surface. A winter estuary is an ideal place to observe feeding methods, and marvel at how the different birds use this amazing resource that, on the face of it, just looks like mud.

While waders scamper over estuarine ooze, an equally impressive array of wildfowl – ducks, geese and swans – slip down from northern wetlands to ply their various trades here on the water, dabbling, up-ending, filtering, diving. Many winter on freshwater lakes and marshes, whilst others spread out over the sea. Both these habitats offer memorable winter birdwatching. Colourful male ducks enliven the dreary, ash-grey waters of inland reservoirs with their breeding finery, and indulge in bouts of courtship, lifting their chins, stretching their bodies, thrusting their heads on to their backs, or whatever might

Great Spotted Woodpecker

spark the passions of a seemingly disinterested female swimming nearby. On the sea various ducks mix with other salt-water users, including divers, grebes and auks, all of them together offering an exciting challenge to a patient watcher. On a windy, choppy sea, these birds give tantalizing glimpses in between waves, barely showing enough to identify themselves. This sea-watching over wild waters, from deserted beaches, using the limits of one's endurance and ability, could be described as birdwatching 'on the edge' – purgatory to some, but curiously addictive to others.

Nobody, no matter what their birdwatching profile, should miss an encounter between December and February with largest of the wildfowl, the swans and geese. These birds come down from the north to a few selected locations at the height of each winter, to places where they can obtain food on agricultural fields during the day, and can then retreat to the safety of large lakes or estuaries to roost at night. These large birds form large flocks, spreading in swarms over fields, or taking to the skies in impressive formations. But it's the sound that they make that turns a spectacle into an experience. Geese might cackle and swans might whoop, but when hundreds of voices come together they seem to make music. Add to this lines of birds flying against the red sky of a dawn or dusk, and you have the quintessence of winter.

BIRDWATCHING IN SPRING

MARCH TO MAY

The winter might seem interminable, but spring hatches plans long before it bursts forth. Garden birds are often paired by the beginning of March, and their singing season is by then already several months old. Certain species, including Grey Herons, Rooks and owls will be incubating eggs before the crocuses fade. Even so, to a birdwatcher spring seems to awaken slowly, then pick up pace through the transitory month of April before reaching its dizzy zenith in the madcap month of May.

Like actors during a change of scene, birds in spring must find their positions before they can stake their claim to a territory and to a mate. For resident species, already living in the area where they will nest, this is comparatively easy. But for migratory birds, the race is on. Species that spent the winter in Africa arrive here in a rush, eager to get to the breeding grounds before their peers. The first tentative arrivals flitting about on a chilly March day might look cold and out of place, but these are the winners; their audacity will ensure them the best territories and the best mates.

Few people can witness the changing season better than a birdwatcher. Each arrival of a new species from the south can be cheered, each song registered as proof of the advance of spring. The first arrivals are Chiffchaffs and Wheatears, making landfall on the South Coast in the early days of March, followed a few days later by Sand Martins, Sandwich Terns and Little Ringed Plovers. The next wave brings Swallows and Blackcaps, then Whitethroats and Yellow Wagtails, and then, by April, hosts of species too numerous to mention. One of the laggards is the Cuckoo, that much heralded but ambivalently welcomed parasite, whose song is rarely heard before the middle of April.

The Cuckoo's song is readily recognizable, but those who seek to learn bird sounds can often be overwhelmed by the jumble of voices heard in the latter half of spring. The best time to pick up songs is, in fact, in early March, when only a dozen or so woodland species are singing, and can be distinguished from one another. Go out with an expert, and be prepared to listen. After many tries, some bird songs will stick in the memory. By May the woodlands will sound like the trading floor of the Stock Market, with dozens of speakers competing for attention on the airwaves, all at once. The ears will be overloaded, unable to take anything in.

Everyone should witness a dawn chorus, not for learning, but for the experience of being overwhelmed by natural sound. The dawn chorus mirrors spring itself, starting

Water Rail

slowly (with a few strands of song from a Skylark, Blackbird or Robin), then building up to a crescendo with the advancing light. At its height, dozens of individuals of twenty or more species will be singing at full intensity. These dawn singers are not being polite, nor are they welcoming the day. They are all males (female birds rarely sing), and they are unambiguously telling other males to keep well away. It's a slanging match, albeit a remarkably tuneful one.

Cuckoo

Spring spreads birdwatching rewards unselectively over the whole countryside, so a visit to the local park can be as satisfying as an expedition to a well-known hotspot. Even so, it is still worth heading for the coast, where newly arrived birds will often be concentrated, having made landfall in the early hours of the morning. These arrivals, busily feeding, will be joined during the day by those species, such as Swallows, birds of prey and certain waders, that choose to migrate in the light. April and May are months when, at the best coastal sites, things can be seen to be changing, not just day by day, but hour by hour. At times birds pop up wherever you look, in the crowded bushes, on open fields, and over the sea.

Few places awaken in spring like a large freshwater marsh. In winter these can be unappealing, birdless places, their few denizens apparently hidden behind a thick screen of endless pale-stemmed reeds. But new growth attracts insects and other invertebrates, offering plentiful food for a range of bird species. A marsh is never an easy place to go birding – the reed screen becomes still thicker in spring – but persistent watchers can glimpse such exciting species as Reed and Sedge Warbler, Garganey, Marsh Harrier, Bearded Reedling and Reed Bunting. And it will be noisy. Marshland birds, unable to locate each other by sight in the dense growth, sing loudly. The rare Bittern, found in just a few places in Britain, makes a deep, sonorous booming sound, audible from well over a mile away in still conditions. The Water Rail makes an alarming, pig-like squeal. And, after a day at a springtime marsh, your ears will still ring with the chatter of warblers long after you have gone home.

The tide of spring shifts birds relentlessly towards breeding, and before the end of May almost every species will be well into production. April and May are key months, often dictating a bird species' fortunes for the next year or two. A cold, wet spring is the very worst prospect, making food hard to find and rendering chicks vulnerable to chill and damp. Fine settled weather, especially with a sprinkling of rain, ensures prosperity for all.

What of our winter birds, those that entrust their non-breeding seasons to our gentle climate? Many hold on with us until April or even May, their departure northwards delayed by the slow onset of spring in high latitudes. They moult into breeding plumage, often looking resplendent, waiting for some cue to set them on their journey. They blend in with the new arrivals and resident species, and together this makes for rich pickings for birdwatchers. May is the month of 'Bird Races', with the aim of seeing the maximum number of species in a twenty-four hour period. With a little planning, it is perfectly possible to see over 100 – testament to the richness of this time of year.

BIRDWATCHING IN SUMMER

JUNE TO AUGUST

For many birds, June is a month of hard labour; the days are long, in every sense. A pair of Great Tits might make about 1,000 caterpillar-collecting expeditions every day to keep their growing young satisfied. A polygamous male Hen Harrier, looking after perhaps three mates and their young, might find himself the provider for ten or more mouths besides his own, and that requires a lot of hunting.

However, for summer visitors, such as Swallows, the long days of June and July are the very lure that draws them here to our northern latitudes in the first place. Extended daylight allows breeding birds to pack more activity into a shorter span, giving them scope to find more food, and bring forth more young, than would otherwise be possible. By coming north, such birds can be more productive more quickly. If our days were as short as equatorial ones, our summer visitors might be tempted to remain behind in Africa. But in their short

but frantic stay, these temporary residents often attempt two, or even three broods, one after the other in quick succession, an exhausting and dangerous schedule.

June sees the hatching out of chicks everywhere. In the garden, brown young Starlings stride over lawns, begging noisily with a buzzing, frothy call. Young Robins, looking unfamiliar without the orange breast of their parents, skulk in herbaceous borders. The trees are full of young tits, yellow-washed, bulk-produced (tits have only one brood, with a dozen or more young) and mostly destined for short lives. Broods of ducklings, feeding on gnats, follow perpetually anxious mothers, living in unrelenting danger amidst the utter tranquillity of village ponds and smooth-flowing rivers. Productivity and death are summer bedfellows.

All around our coasts colonies of seabirds will be seething with activity, making a late spring visit an experience not to miss. Be warned, though, large seabird colonies can be overwhelming. They are smelly, noisy, and so full of movement that the eyes will need to get

Gannet with chick

used to the big picture before the individual cameos can be seen and appreciated. No one should rush their time here. Take a flask of coffee, sit and watch. After an hour or so, patterns will emerge and the behaviour of the birds can be understood better. Pairs will meet, bicker with neighbours, fight off intruders, watch for danger and, of course, tend to the needs of their eggs or chicks. Remember, too, that this is reality, not TV. If a predatory bird attacks and takes a chick, this is real death, a life lost, a catastrophe for the parents who have invested everything they have in getting into condition, pairing or reacquainting, producing and laying eggs, incubating and feeding, all until this moment of savage loss.

Our islands are renowned for their seabird colonies (we have, for example, more breeding pairs of Puffins in Britain than of Collared Doves). And there are plenty to choose from – gull colonies on dunes and cliffs; tern colonies on beaches, islands and shingle; Cormorants, auks and Gannet colonies on sea-stacks and cliffs. They are all fantastic. Sea-cliffs offer the best variety, with lots of species sharing the ledges. Different species will be at different stages of their breeding cycle (within a species, breeding tends to be synchronized), so you will be able to see nests, eggs, young chicks and young almost ready to fly, all at the same time. Colonies on beaches and low islands can sometimes be more accessible than cliffs, and you have the chance of being attacked by an irate tern or perhaps a skua, with these bolder birds clipping your scalp and adding the sense of touch to your already-assaulted eyes, ears and nose.

Don't wait until August to visit the seabird cliffs, because by then the short breeding season will be over, and many of the nesting species will have already left. Whole colonies of Puffins, for example, disappear within the space of a few late summer days, then swim out to sea. One day they are there, the next they are gone. The cliffs they leave behind will have the look of a deserted stadium after a match.

By then the wider countryside, too, will have a winding-down feel. Although many species will still be breeding, the business of singing will have run its course, and territorial boundaries will have broken down under the patter of itinerant fledglings' feet. Instead, there is now a great shedding of feathers, as birds everywhere undertake their main annual moult, and generally keep a low profile. The garden suddenly seems to be a very quiet place, as birds devote their energies to their change of plumage, and skulk in the undergrowth.

Late summer is a confusing time of year for birdwatchers. With moulting adults everywhere, and young birds presenting various different plumages and making unusual calls, this is a time for patient note-taking and putting up with identification defeats nobly. Duck species, in particular, make life difficult, because the colourful drakes change for the late summer into what is known as 'eclipse' plumage, a cryptic, female-like mode of dress that affords them camouflage while they are moulting their flight feathers. They become very difficult to tell apart both from their females and from all the other duck species.

Migrant birds often make the most cursory of visits to their breeding quarters. Swifts, having deigned to arrive in Britain only in May, have all but deserted the country by the end of August, and hot on their heels come Pied Flycatchers and Nightingales, the latter having entertained us with their thrilling songs only fleetingly. These are headline names among a number of species that begin their migration southward at the time the hot months of summer take hold.

Unexpectedly, perhaps, it is necessary to go back to the end of June to encounter the very first returnees. These are waders who, for various reasons, have failed to breed. Their departures from their breeding grounds can even coincide with the last of certain northbound arrivals of various species still hoping for nesting success. These waders are the vanguard, just the trickle that signals the great southbound rush that reaches its peak in autumn.

Goldfinch on teasel

BIRDWATCHING IN AUTUMN

SEPTEMBER TO NOVEMBER

If birds seem to be everywhere in autumn, that's because they are everywhere. Populations are at peak levels because the breeding season just past has added large numbers of youngsters to the melting pot. And birds are showing themselves; they have a restless feel, feeding up for migration, preparing for the winter. Some are already on the move.

The season's youngsters are often called 'first-winters,' because these rookie birds are exhibiting the adult-like plumage that they will wear for their first winter of life, not the special 'leave me alone' plumage of their juvenile days. Most are immediately plunged into an unforgiving world. Some must feed up and migrate thousands of miles, completely unaided, to wintering areas they have never seen. Others will stay put, but enter a life-and-death struggle for a territory. Tawny Owls, for example, must

fight for a patch where they can learn to catch food to survive the winter; if they don't succeed they will die. Robins, as violent as they are attractive, spend much of the autumn at loggerheads, and there are many casualties.

With so many birds migrating, the autumn serves up a daily dose of excitement and anticipation for birdwatchers. Once again, as in spring, the coast offers particular riches, especially when inclement weather conspires to bring large numbers of individuals of many species down into one small area. This phenomenon is known as a 'fall' of migrants, and one of the best places to observe one is on an island or at a headland. Many such places are home to a bird observatory, where birds are caught and ringed (metal identification rings put on their legs) to aid the study of their migration patterns and population levels. Aim to spend some time at one, and you will get a feel for the excitement engendered by the unpredictability of bird movements. Follow one of the observatory staff making their rounds of the mist-nets, and the experience will have the feel of a 'lucky dip'. Who knows of what species the next wriggling sprite will be?

Young birds are singularly prone to migratory mishaps, and over the last fifty years a remarkable number of species of birds have been seen in Britain in autumn that really ought not to be here. Birds blunder over from all directions, from America in the west to Siberia in the east. This has spawned a lively interest in rare birds in Britain, which has, comparatively recently, developed into an offshoot of birdwatching called 'twitching.'

Twitching, in effect, is gathering a personal list of birds seen. Once the common birds have been ticked off, only the rarities are left, so twitchers must follow up on bird news and travel countrywide to effect appointments with their desired species. Every birdwatcher should join at least one 'twitch', if only to enjoy the twitchers themselves and their infectious enthusiasm.

Autumn might be a time of change and strife for birds, but it does at least offer a super-abundance of food just about everywhere. The insect bloom is by no means over, and with herbs seeding, trees fruiting and bushes and shrubs producing explosions of berries, there is no excuse not to prosper. Birdwatchers should be drawn to berries, too, for a large number of species subsist upon them, from outgoing Garden Warblers to incoming Redwings. A berry-bearing Elder, for example, is like a bird table, a stationary resource with lots of visitors. Aim to spend an hour or two just sitting by a berry-rich hedgerow, and watch the waves of birds come and go.

Some species of birds have particularly strong relationships with the plants upon which they feed. Jays spend much of the autumn collecting acorns, several thousand of which each bird secretes away in as many secret burial places, to be retrieved on a lean, winter day. Some acorns get forgotten or left, and many of these, quite naturally, grow to become oak trees. Mistle Thrushes become positively stingy about Holly trees or Mistletoe clumps, keeping all birds away from their personal living larders with aggressive, security-guard fervour. Goldfinches, as enthusiastic about thistles as gardeners hate them, stuff themselves with late-setting thistle seeds, and feed them to young that might have hatched as late as August.

By November, even the riches of autumn begin to dwindle, and the hours of daylight drain away. It's the slide towards winter, so the last migrants must absolutely be on their way. Even so, there are always records of Wheatears and Swallows in November, hurrying south to an uncertain fate.

In summer, the activities of the day are uppermost in a bird's considerations, but now, in late autumn, far more attention is given to surviving the long nights. To beat the night requires a two-pronged strategy – finding enough food by day, and securing a reliable roosting place, with adequate shelter and protection from predators, for the hours of darkness. To get either wrong will inevitably be fatal.

Although birds obviously sleep during the summer, their activity around roosting sites is always far more obvious in autumn and winter. Blackbirds make loud 'chinking' noises as they testily sort out who sleeps where amidst the branches of trees; gulls fly in impressive V-formations on their way to lakes and reservoirs; and Jackdaws, Rooks and crows indulge in shouting matches well into the night as the ownership of choice positions is constantly challenged. Many species of birds choose to roost in groups, partly for the communal awareness of predators, partly to observe the health of others (and assess their feeding activities), and partly because good sites are at a premium.

Starlings are famed for their communal roosts, not just for the noise they make during the night, but also for their remarkable pre-roost aerobatics, in which thousands of birds often take part, and whirl across the sky in mass movements that resemble plumes of smoke, or some curious amoeboid organism. It is another sight and sound that a birdwatcher mustn't miss, especially if it can be viewed against the background of a setting sun. It only lasts for a few short minutes, until the night banishes such high spirits and fixes its stern grip upon one and all.

Rooks feeding

JANUARY

Magpies

MAIN EVENTS

- Good numbers of birds come to the garden.

- Most birds are established in their winter quarters.

- Cold conditions bring 'hard-weather movements', with many birds fleeing the frost and snow, and appearing almost anywhere.

- Many birds begin to sing, especially tits. Woodpeckers begin to drum.

- If long periods of frost prevail, many small species such as Wrens, Long-tailed Tits and Dartford Warblers will suffer substantial losses. Kingfishers and Grey Herons, too, will find their feeding areas frozen over.

- Many birds can be seen at communal roosts, including Starlings, crows, finches and Hen Harriers.

- A few birds might even be nesting, among them Crossbills and Ring-necked Parakeets.

- The first seabirds, such as Guillemots, begin to show interest in their nesting cliffs.

WHERE TO GO AND WHAT TO LOOK FOR

Visit a muddy estuary, such as the Severn Estuary, to see large numbers of waders.

Find a large harbour or shallow coast, and watch for seaducks, divers and grebes on the water.

Reservoirs are worth visiting for large numbers of wildfowl.

Impressive flocks of wild geese can be seen in many parts of Britain, including Norfolk, Lancashire, the Solway and the island of Islay.

Look for Snow Buntings and Twite on salt marshes and dunes.

JANUARY

Siskin

Fieldfare

Robin

Waxwing

SEASONAL SUGGESTION

Whenever you go out bird-watching, always put on one more layer of clothing than you think you will need. Wear a warm hat and gloves. Most people also find that walking boots are better than wellingtons in cold weather.

Siskin

Fieldfare

Robin

Waxwing

SEASONAL SUGGESTION

Birds do not like snow and ice, but these conditions provide interesting birdwatching. Look for flocks of Lapwings, Golden Plovers, thrushes and Skylarks flying over to escape the bad weather.

Siskin

Fieldfare

Robin

Waxwing

SEASONAL SUGGESTION

Periods of sharp cold often bring unusual birds to the country. Watch for geese flying high over, or for wandering birds of prey, and check every bird in winter flocks carefully.

JANUARY

Siskin

Fieldfare

Robin

Waxwing

SEASONAL SUGGESTION

The best birdwatchers go to one particular place regularly to see how bird numbers vary throughout the year, and observe how birds behave at different times. If you haven't already got one, find your own 'local patch'.

JANUARY

Siskin

Fieldfare

Robin

Waxwing

SEASONAL SUGGESTION

On an estuary, be wise to the tides. Time your visit to coincide an hour or two before and after high tide. High tides bring birds closer into view, and cause much milling about.

JANUARY

Siskin

Fieldfare

Robin

Waxwing

FEBRUARY

Rookery in winter

MAIN EVENTS

- Long-tailed Tits begin nest-building towards the end of the month. Watch for them in the morning, collecting moss, lichen, cobwebs or feathers.

- Interesting birds often start to appear in the garden in February, especially Siskins.

- Blackbirds and Chaffinches begin singing.

- A few species including Grey Herons, Rooks and Ravens begin nest-building.

- Duck numbers build up on many reservoirs and lakes.

- It's a good month to observe ducks displaying on the water.

- Gulls begin to acquire their summer plumage with, for example, Black-headed Gulls gaining brown hoods.

- Birds of prey, including Merlin, Peregrine and Hen Harrier can be seen almost anywhere where flocks of birds are found.

WHERE TO GO AND WHAT TO LOOK FOR

Head for any one of the Wildfowl & Wetlands Trust Centres, especially those that attract wild swans, for example Slimbridge, Welney, and Martin Mere.

Visit a heronry or a rookery to watch the birds' greeting displays and nest-building.

Estuaries, reservoirs and coastal regions, such as South Walney in Cumbria and Grafham Water in Cambridgeshire, remain good sites for birdwatching, just as they are in January.

FEBRUARY

Siskin

Fieldfare

Robin

Waxwing

SEASONAL SUGGESTION

In February, when the light is low and the days short, it is essential to make sure your binocular lenses are kept clean at all times. Use a soft lens cloth, available from any camera shop.

FEBRUARY

Siskin

Fieldfare

Robin

Waxwing

SEASONAL SUGGESTION

Dark, cloudy conditions make birds look larger, so be aware of this when estimating the size of a bird.

FEBRUARY

Siskin

Fieldfare

Robin

Waxwing

SEASONAL SUGGESTION

Don't forget to include counts in your notes. Counting birds is difficult, and it's not always appropriate to cover each bird individually. Try counting birds in multiples, such as 3s, 5s or 10s.

FEBRUARY

Siskin

Fieldfare

Robin

Waxwing

SEASONAL SUGGESTION

Try to remain quiet when you are birdwatching, especially when approaching or leaving a hide. Wild geese and ducks will fly away if they detect the slightest disturbance.

FEBRUARY

Siskin

Fieldfare

Robin

Waxwing

SEASONAL SUGGESTION

When birdwatching, wear sober colours, and clothing that does not rustle too much. This especially applies when visiting open habitats, such as wetlands and the coast.

FEBRUARY

Siskin

Fieldfare

Robin

Waxwing

MARCH

*Male and
female Bullfinch*

MAIN EVENTS

🐦 The first summer migrants including Chiffchaffs, Little Ringed Plovers, Wheatears, Sand Martins and Sandwich Terns appear, usually on the South Coast.

🐦 The first migrant intruders on the bird song scene will be Chiffchaffs singing their name.

🐦 Great Crested Grebes perform their incomparable displays on freshwater lakes.

🐦 On sunny days, Sparrowhawks display over woods, soaring then describing a huge U-shape with a dive and a lift.

🐦 Mistle Thrushes are incubating their eggs. It is the earliest of our thrushes to nest.

🐦 Watch for the aerial displays of pigeons and doves in suburban areas.

🐦 Look for Bullfinches on your buds in the garden – beautiful but destructive.

🐦 Redwings gather together and make communal babbling noises, a prelude to their departure.

WHERE TO GO AND WHAT TO LOOK FOR

Visit the South Coast of England for early returning migrants such as Wheatears.

A gravel pit or reservoir should attract returning migrants, especially Sand Martins.

This is a good month to visit any woodland, where many resident species will be singing, and are visible.

MARCH

Bullfinches

Kingfisher

Nightingale

Cuckoo

SEASONAL SUGGESTION

This is a good month to learn bird song, with the use of a companion cassette or CD because, although the resident birds are in full cry, not many migrant birds have arrived to confuse the issue.

Bullfinches

Kingfisher

Nightingale

Cuckoo

SEASONAL SUGGESTION

March is great for birdwatching by the riverside. The soft light of an early spring day offsets the bright or bold colours of Kingfisher, Grey Wagtail and Dipper.

MARCH

Bullfinches

Kingfisher

Nightingale

Cuckoo

SEASONAL SUGGESTION

Often, the key to finding a bird of prey, such as a Sparrowhawk, is to monitor the reaction of the birds around it. Look for angrily calling crows on the horizon, or swirling flocks of Starlings and pigeons. When birds see a predator, they also make high-pitched, drawn-out calls (known as 'hawk alarm calls') which you can learn to recognize.

MARCH

Bullfinches

Kingfisher

Nightingale

Cuckoo

SEASONAL SUGGESTION

March is a good month for woodland birdwatching, because the birds are noisy and active before the leaves are on the trees. Many scarce species, such as Hawfinches and Lesser Spotted Woodpeckers, are best looked for at this time.

MARCH

Bullfinches

Kingfisher

Nightingale

Cuckoo

SEASONAL SUGGESTION

When birdwatching, be careful not to point at a bird, especially one that is nearby. Rapid movements frighten birds. And when in a hide, never point through the viewing window.

MARCH

Bullfinches

Kingfisher

Nightingale

Cuckoo

APRIL

Song Thrush

MAIN EVENTS

- Waves of migrants arrive from Africa all month long. Species include Yellow Wagtails, Tree Pipits, Swallows, Blackcaps, Willow Warblers and Whitethroats.

- The first Cuckoo utters its unmistakable song.

- Ospreys arrive in Scotland and, nowadays, England, too.

- Resident birds are all breeding. Many already have eggs, and the early nesters are feeding young.

- The number of seaduck in Scotland is at its peak.

- Ring Ouzels head for their upland territories, and often stop off on hills and cliffs on the way.

- The last winter visitors, including Fieldfares, Redwings and Bramblings, usually depart. They sometimes sing as a parting farewell.

WHERE TO GO AND WHAT TO LOOK FOR

It's a good time to visit an estuary. Here you will get the chance to see waders in their colourful breeding plumage. Grey Plovers, Knots and Turnstones are all stunning.

If you can, visit Central Scotland for the communal display (lek) of a Capercaillie.

Try a northern coastal area, such as Spey Bay, Scotland, for seaducks in fine plumage and at their noisiest.

APRIL

Swallow

Bullfinches

Kingfisher

Nightingale

Cuckoo

SEASONAL SUGGESTION

Have you ever seen an owl? If not, listen for the 'chink' calls of Blackbirds, especially if uttered by day, and the ensuing disturbance. The cause will often be an owl.

APRIL

Swallow

Bullfinches

Kingfisher

Nightingale

Cuckoo

SEASONAL SUGGESTION

Spring is the time when all birds are in their most colourful plumage, and when males and females look most different from each other. It's a good time to enjoy your birds before wear and moult and youngsters cloud the issue.

APRIL

Swallow

Bullfinches

Kingfisher

Nightingale

Cuckoo

SEASONAL SUGGESTION

April showers are notorious, so make sure your binoculars are fitted with rain-caps. Also, if you do get the lenses wet, be careful when wiping them; smearing water all over them can render them useless for short periods of time.

APRIL

Swallow

Bullfinches

Kingfisher

Nightingale

Cuckoo

SEASONAL SUGGESTION

When listening to birds, it is often a very good idea to cup your hands behind your ears, and stand facing the source of the sound. This not only helps to magnify the sound, but will also help you pinpoint more accurately where the bird is.

APRIL

Swallow

Bullfinches

Kingfisher

Nightingale

Cuckoo

SEASONAL SUGGESTION

A very good rule for all birdwatchers is to get to know the most common species thoroughly. So try to observe our commoner birds in lots of weather conditions, light and different plumage, and become completely familiar with them. Then identifying more unusual species will become easier.

APRIL

Swallow

Bullfinches

Kingfisher

Nightingale

Cuckoo

MAY

Chiffchaff

MAIN EVENTS

🐦 The spring migration continues apace, with new birds arriving daily.

🐦 Swifts and Garden Warblers make their first appearance.

🐦 Almost every bird is singing or performing visual displays.

🐦 Much breeding activity can be seen everywhere.

🐦 Nightingales are singing, just for this month and the first two weeks of June.

🐦 Pipits are performing their impressive 'parachuting' displays.

🐦 Larks can begin singing as early as 2.30am.

🐦 Colourful Continental visitors such as Hoopoes, Golden Orioles and Bee-eaters sometimes 'overshoot' and reach Britain.

🐦 Grey Heron juveniles will begin learning to fish.

🐦 House Martins will be collecting mud to build their nests.

🐦 There is a strong passage of several waders, including Whimbrels, Sanderlings and Bar-tailed Godwits.

WHERE TO GO AND WHAT TO LOOK FOR

It's a great month for exploring the Highlands of Scotland.

Nightingales are found in thickets only in south-east England. They are very localized, so it is probably best to join a local bird club on a special 'Nightingale Trip'.

Try the Sessile Oakwoods of Wales for breeding Redstarts, Pied Flycatchers and Wood Warblers.

MAY

Swallow

Bullfinches

Kingfisher

Nightingale

Cuckoo

SEASONAL SUGGESTION

This is the month to get up early, not just to witness the dawn chorus, but also to watch for any incoming birds that have been migrating overnight.

MAY

Swallow

Bullfinches

Kingfisher

Nightingale

Cuckoo

SEASONAL SUGGESTION

May is probably the best month for birdwatching in Britain: the birds are in bright plumage, they are singing, and there is a greater variety of species around than in any other month. Spend lots of time out in the field.

MAY

Swallow

Bullfinches

Kingfisher

Nightingale

Cuckoo

SEASONAL SUGGESTION

May is a good month to test your concentration. When there are lots of birds around, it's easy to be 'butterfly-minded', flitting from one bird to another and being easily distracted. But the best birdwatchers maintain their concentration and attention to detail.

MAY

Swallow

Bullfinches

Kingfisher

Nightingale

Cuckoo

SEASONAL SUGGESTION

When trying to recognize bird songs, don't forget to let the bird finish its sentence before you identify it. Learning songs is hard enough without trying to pick up mere snatches. The Song Thrush, for example, has a slow-paced but highly varied song. However, this thrush's opening phrases are often identified as another bird's before it's had time to declare its identity.

Swallow

Bullfinches

Kingfisher

Nightingale

Cuckoo

MAY

SEASONAL SUGGESTION

Try to learn only the common songs at first. About three quarters of all the songs and calls you hear throughout the year will be from a handful of species: Blue Tit, Great Tit, Wren, Dunnock, Robin, Blackbird, Song Thrush, Mistle Thrush and Chaffinch.

Swallow

Bullfinches

Kingfisher

Nightingale

Cuckoo

JUNE

Swifts over rooftops

MAIN EVENTS

- For most birds the breeding season is in full swing. Nests and young are everywhere.

- The very last summer visitors arrive, including Spotted Flycatcher, Turtle Dove and the rare Marsh Warbler.

- The garden lawn will play host to recently fledged, brown young Starlings.

- This is the month when the first – and only – broods of tits leave the nest.

- Some of Britain's most secretive birds are singing, including Spotted Crake, Corncrake and Quail.

- Sedge Warblers virtually stop singing, whilst Reed Warblers tend to continue.

- This is a good month to hear Grasshopper Warbler.

WHERE TO GO AND WHAT TO LOOK FOR

Choose a still day and visit a large freshwater marsh, such as Brandon Marsh in Coventry, Doxey Marshes in Staffordshire, Minsmere in Suffolk or Stodmarsh in Kent.

Visit a seabird colony, such as Handa Island in Scotland, either this month or in July.

Visit a high moorland. You'll be overwhelmed, not only by the scenery, but also by the fantastic sounds of Curlew, Snipe and Lapwing.

The New Forest, in Hampshire, is well worth a visit with its very special set of breeding birds, including Honey Buzzard.

JUNE

Nightjar

Turtle Dove

Hobby

Skylark

Spotted
Flycatcher

SEASONAL SUGGESTION

June is a good month to look for elusive birds; they will be busily feeding young and will make less effort than usual to conceal themselves. Examples include the Bittern, which usually hides in reedbeds, and the various owl species, which can often be seen by day at this time of year.

JUNE

Nightjar

Turtle Dove

Hobby

Skylark

Spotted
Flycatcher

SEASONAL SUGGESTION

There is often something of a lull in bird activity in the second half of June. Migration has ended, and many birds are in between broods. So now is a good time to get to know your local patch better while enjoying the weather.

JUNE

Nightjar

Turtle Dove

Hobby

Skylark

Spotted
Flycatcher

SEASONAL SUGGESTION

Birds are most active at daybreak and dusk, something that is never more obvious than in June.

JUNE

Nightjar

Turtle Dove

Hobby

Skylark

*Spotted
Flycatcher*

SEASONAL SUGGESTION

June is a 'sit-and-wait' month as birds are mostly active in the vicinity of their nests. You will find it more rewarding to sit on the ground, or in a hide, and wait for birds to come to you, than to walk around.

JUNE

Nightjar

Turtle Dove

Hobby

Skylark

Spotted
Flycatcher

SEASONAL SUGGESTION

If you go Nightjar hunting in June or July, take a white handkerchief. Waving it is said to attract male Nightjars, which mistake the handkerchief for the white wing-patches on a rival male.

JUNE

Nightjar

Turtle Dove

Hobby

Skylark

Spotted Flycatcher

JULY

Woodpigeons

MAIN EVENTS

- Many young birds leave their families and disperse, often finding their way to unexpected places. This is a good month for unusual birds in the garden.

- Many birds are starting their second broods.

- In the countryside, the main breeding season for Woodpigeons and House Sparrows is just beginning.

- The Hobby, a dashing bird of prey, begins to breed. It times its activities so that the young can be fed on the abundant young Swifts and Swallows that will fill the skies in the next month or two.

- The countryside is quiet of song, except for the persistent 'Little-bit-of-bread-and-no-cheese' ditty of the Yellowhammer.

- The first 'autumn migrants' arrive on our wetlands. These are waders from the Arctic that have failed to breed.

- Ducklings appear on rivers and lakes.

- In certain years, Crossbills turn up in coniferous woods where they are not normally seen.

WHERE TO GO AND WHAT TO LOOK FOR

Visit a seabird colony, either on a cliff or a low island or sandbank.

At dusk, take a torch and go to a lowland heath or moor such as Redmoor near Bodmin or Brownsea Island in Poole. This will give you the chance to hear the strange, hollow 'churring' of a Nightjar. Local clubs often arrange special Nightjar trips.

July is an excellent month to visit mountainous areas. For example, in the Cairngorms, Ptarmigan, Snow Bunting and Dotterel can be found. On other mountains, look for Golden Plovers, Ring Ouzels and Twite.

JULY

Nightjar

Turtle Dove

Hobby

Skylark

Spotted
Flycatcher

SEASONAL SUGGESTION

When birdwatching on a sunny day, try to keep in the shade. You will be more difficult to see, and as a result you'll get closer to the birds.

JULY

Nightjar

Turtle Dove

Hobby

Skylark

Spotted
Flycatcher

SEASONAL SUGGESTION

Try to use sunshine to
your advantage. Make sure
the light is behind you
when watching birds.
Remember, too, that the
light can play tricks,
making dark colours seem
pale, and birds seem larger.

JULY

Nightjar

Turtle Dove

Hobby

Skylark

Spotted
Flycatcher

SEASONAL SUGGESTION

Many birds seem to disappear in July, especially in the garden. This is because they become quiet and less active as the main annual moult approaches.

JULY

Nightjar

Turtle Dove

Hobby

Skylark

*Spotted
Flycatcher*

SEASONAL SUGGESTION

To find birds in July, look for water. Any pool, gravel pit, sewage farm and lake will be alive with birds feeding, bathing and drinking, while the surrounding woodlands and fields seem empty.

JULY

Nightjar

Turtle Dove

Hobby

Skylark

Spotted
Flycatcher

AUGUST

Starlings and Black-headed Gulls

MAIN EVENTS

- Most birds undergo their main annual moult.

- Young birds often gather in large, mixed-species flocks that roam along hedgerows and woodlands.

- Some adult birds make an early departure from their breeding areas, beginning their long migration and leaving the young behind. The most obvious example is the Cuckoo.

- All the Swifts, Pied Flycatchers and Nightingales leave us.

- The annual British Birdwatching Fair takes place at Rutland Water.

- The hatching out of flying ants takes place on certain warm days. Watch for excited flocks of birds whirling in the sky.

- The last week of August is usually when the juvenile waders appear in numbers from their Arctic hatching grounds.

- Shelducks all but disappear from Britain, going off to moult on the seas off North Germany. Some, however, visit Bridgwater Bay in Somerset.

WHERE TO GO AND WHAT TO LOOK FOR

Find a sheltered coastal lagoon, or inland gravel pit – anywhere with extensive, undisturbed mud. It's a marvellous time for observing waders in many different plumages.

It's a good month to start sea-watching, so find a piece of land that juts out into the sea. Manx Shearwaters should feature.

Try any area of scrub or hedgerow near you. Mixed flocks of young birds, often led by Long-tailed Tits, should make an appearance.

Turtle Dove

Hobby

Skylark

Spotted
Flycatcher

SEASONAL SUGGESTION

August can be a good month for watching birds of prey, which make the most of the summer thermals. Wait for a sunny day, with a light breeze and some cumulus cloud, and watch the sky. Don't start until at least 10.00am, as the birds are waiting for the thermals to form.

AUGUST

Turtle Dove

Hobby

Skylark

Spotted
Flycatcher

SEASONAL SUGGESTION

This is a month of tricky plumages. Young birds usually sport a different plumage from the adults, for example the juvenile Robin lacks a red breast, and young swans are brown. So take special care when identifying birds.

AUGUST

Turtle Dove

Hobby

Skylark

Spotted
Flycatcher

SEASONAL SUGGESTION

All the ducks look brown at the moment, the males having moulted into a special female-like plumage known as 'eclipse'. So, if you want a challenge, go to a marsh or lake and try identifying the duck species.

AUGUST

Turtle Dove

Hobby

Skylark

Spotted
Flycatcher

SEASONAL SUGGESTION

Concentrating on watching birds and looking into bright skies can be bad for your health. Wear a sun hat and bring lots of water with you when birdwatching on a hot day.

AUGUST

Turtle Dove

Hobby

Skylark

*Spotted
Flycatcher*

SEASONAL SUGGESTION

Many birdwatchers consider the 20th August to signal the start of the main autumn migration.

AUGUST

Turtle Dove

Hobby

Skylark

Spotted
Flycatcher

SEPTEMBER

Garden Warbler

MAIN EVENTS

- The autumn migration is at its peak. Millions of birds are on their way southwards, either departing for Africa, or arriving from northern and Central Europe.

- Swallows are gathering on wires.

- Any bed of thistles will attract Goldfinches, including late-brood youngsters that have just left the nest.

- Birds everywhere are feeding feverishly, either during migration or in preparation for it.

- The last Cuckoos leave, all of which are youngsters.

- The bulk of the populations of many species leave us in September, including Willow Warblers and Sedge Warblers.

- Birds such as Whinchats, Redstarts, Garden Warblers and Wheatears can be seen almost everywhere.

- Skuas and shearwaters are passing offshore.

WHERE TO GO AND WHAT TO LOOK FOR

Migrants are usually easiest to see on the coast, so aim to get there in September if you can.

Choose a high point looking over the sea, and an onshore wind, and watch for passing seabirds. It's best to start at dawn.

Visit any bird observatory, where migratory birds are studied and ringed.

Muddy spots will fill up with waders. This is the best time of the year to see Little Stints and Curlew Sandpipers.

SEPTEMBER

Spotted Redshank

Jays

Goldfinches

SEASONAL SUGGESTION

Rain or fog often grounds migrating birds, so it can be worth a visit to the coast if such conditions are predicted in the morning.

SEPTEMBER

Spotted Redshank

Jays

Goldfinches

SEASONAL SUGGESTION

In September and October, look for berries and you will find birds. The larger the berry, the larger the bird. Elderberry bushes and Haws attract a great variety of customers.

SEPTEMBER

Spotted Redshank

Jays

Goldfinches

SEASONAL SUGGESTION

Birds, especially migrating birds, seek out places that are sheltered from the wind but touched by the sun. Treetops, and places where sun and shadow meet, are worth checking.

SEPTEMBER

Spotted Redshank

Jays

Goldfinches

SEASONAL SUGGESTION

Not many birds are singing in September, but Robins are. Lots of birds are calling, that is making one- or two-syllable sounds in response to situations such as alarm, but only Robins are declaring ownership of a territory with complex phrases and 'sentences'. Go into a wood right now and Robins will be everywhere.

SEPTEMBER

Spotted Redshank

Jays

Goldfinches

SEASONAL SUGGESTION

If you've never tried it, September is the best month to try 'sea-watching'. Take your binoculars or, preferably, a telescope; find a comfortable spot overlooking the sea, and sit patiently, watching for the occasional dot to pass over the waves. This is a good month for skuas and shearwaters.

NOTES

Spotted Redshank

Jays

Goldfinches

OCTOBER

Jay

MAIN EVENTS

- The autumn migration is still in full swing, and many rare and unusual birds appear throughout the country.

- It is the peak season for daytime movement with incoming Starlings, larks, pipits, finches and pigeons.

- Thousands of waders and wildfowl arrive.

- The first wild geese, including Brent Geese, turn up at their winter haunts.

- Jays are everywhere, moving around in small groups looking for acorns.

- Thrushes arrive from the continent. Among their number are the 'Winter Thrushes', Redwings and Fieldfares. All of them gorge upon berries.

- The last of many species of migrants can be seen, including Lesser Whitethroats, Blackcaps, House Martins and Chiffchaffs.

- Many skuas and other seabirds continue to pass offshore.

WHERE TO GO AND WHAT TO LOOK FOR

Visit the East Coast of England or Scotland, where exciting migrants from the nearby continent make first landfall. Norfolk is especially recommended.

A celebrated October location is The Wildlife Trusts' most recent member, the Isles of Scilly, off Cornwall, where extraordinary numbers of rare birds turn up every year, along with an incredible variety of more common species.

Visit an oak wood to enjoy the antics of the Jays.

OCTOBER

Arctic Skua

Spotted Redshank

Jays

Goldfinches

SEASONAL SUGGESTION

This is a good month to go outside at night, especially if it is clear. Redwings and Fieldfares migrate at night, and you can hear them flying over almost anywhere. In the woods, owls can be heard.

OCTOBER

Arctic Skua

Spotted Redshank

Jays

Goldfinches

SEASONAL SUGGESTION

Watch the weather in October. East winds often bring exciting birds into Britain.

OCTOBER

Arctic Skua

Spotted Redshank

Jays

Goldfinches

SEASONAL SUGGESTION

This is a good month to keep your eyes to the sky. Many species migrate during the day in October, making upward glances rewarding.

OCTOBER

Arctic Skua

Spotted Redshank

Jays

Goldfinches

SEASONAL SUGGESTION

If you hear a steady, slow-paced tapping when you walk through a wood, it could be a woodpecker working a piece of dead wood, or it could be a Nuthatch, Marsh Tit or Great Tit tapping at a nut.

OCTOBER

Arctic Skua

Spotted Redshank

Jays

Goldfinches

SEASONAL SUGGESTION

It can be difficult to find birds through binoculars, especially if the former are moving. When transferring from sight to optics, make sure that you never take your eyes off the bird; simply look at it and raise your binoculars quickly upwards, without looking down. Try practising this technique on falling autumn leaves.

OCTOBER

Arctic Skua

Spotted Redshank

Jays

Goldfinches

NOVEMBER

Goldcrest

MAIN EVENTS

- The autumn migration tails off. The very last summer visitors, such as Swallows and Wheatears, tend to be seen in the first week.

- Song Thrush and Mistle Thrush begin to sing.

- Bramblings are in Beechwoods.

- Birds tend to disappear from uplands and mountainous areas.

- Snow Buntings, Twites and even Shore Larks and Lapland Bunting have settled in to winter on dunes and salt marshes.

- Unusual gulls, such as Iceland Gull and Glaucous Gull, begin to make an appearance.

WHERE TO GO AND WHAT TO LOOK FOR

Why not pay a visit to Central Wales and sites such as The Wildlife Trusts' reserve at Gilfach Farm to see the Red Kites and other birds of prey? There are several special feeding stations where large numbers of kites come in to be fed at dusk.

This is a good time of year to visit a Starling roost, and watch the comings and goings of the birds.

It's a good time to look for Water Pipits, at sewage farms, cress beds and damp pasture.

On Firework Night, try listening for Redwings flying overhead in the darkness.

NOVEMBER

Spotted Redshank

Jays

Goldfinches

SEASONAL SUGGESTION

It's often windy in November, and the birds are no more keen on these conditions than you are. When birdwatching in such weather, seek out sheltered places, such as hollows, bushes behind walls, and harbours.

NOVEMBER

Spotted Redshank

Jays

Goldfinches

SEASONAL SUGGESTION

Many birds favour certain types of trees, making them easier to track down. In winter, Siskins and Goldfinches feed in riverside alders, while Redpolls prefer birches. Chaffinches and Bramblings like beechwoods, and Hawfinches are especially partial to hornbeams.

NOVEMBER

Spotted Redshank

Jays

Goldfinches

SEASONAL SUGGESTION

Autumn storms, especially with west or north-west winds, often bring exciting birds to exposed coasts.

NOVEMBER

Spotted Redshank

Jays

Goldfinches

**SEASONAL
SUGGESTION**

A simple rule of
birdwatching in winter
woodlands is to keep
checking the treetops.
Many birds use them
as lookouts.

NOVEMBER

Spotted Redshank

Jays

Goldfinches

SEASONAL SUGGESTION

There are always more species on the edge of a habitat, where it adjoins another, such as woodland next to a field, or a marsh moving into scrub, than in the pure habitat itself. So your most productive birdwatching will be in a tapestry of different habitats.

NOVEMBER

Spotted Redshank

Jays

Goldfinches

DECEMBER

Redwing

MAIN EVENTS

- Most birds have settled into their winter haunts.
- Periods of extreme cold in the Near Continent often force waves of birds to come into Britain.
- Bean Geese arrive in certain parts of the country.
- Bewick's Swans also appear.
- In the garden, the first Robins begin to pair up.
- On fast-flowing streams, Dippers begin to sing and establish territories.
- Gatherings of Pied Wagtails often roost on large municipal Christmas trees, taking advantage of the warmth of fairy lights.

WHERE TO GO AND WHAT TO LOOK FOR

Estuaries are full with their winter populations of waders, so a visit will be profitable.

Any reservoir or lake will have good populations of ducks and grebes.

A good month to look for Smew, mainly on reservoirs and gravel pits in south-east England.

Siskin

Fieldfare

Robin

Waxwing

DECEMBER

SEASONAL SUGGESTION

Woodland often appears lifeless in December, but be patient. Most birds are moving around in flocks, and you are bound to stumble upon one of these eventually.

DECEMBER

Siskin

Fieldfare

Robin

Waxwing

SEASONAL SUGGESTION

December is a good month to use the long evenings for study. If you've never done it before, get out your field guide and have a good look through it. You'll be amazed what you learn.

DECEMBER

Siskin

Fieldfare

Robin

Waxwing

SEASONAL SUGGESTION

It's difficult to concentrate when you're cold and uncomfortable, so make sure you wear warm, comfortable clothing. Take a good pair of gloves, not mittens, as these will make it difficult to focus your binoculars, and, if necessary, bring some hand-warmers.

DECEMBER

Siskin

Fieldfare

Robin

Waxwing

SEASONAL SUGGESTION

On the mud-flats, different predators will produce different reactions. Few birds will fly up at the appearance of a Kestrel, but if a Merlin or Sparrowhawk appears, all the smaller birds, including waders, gulls and some ducks will scatter. If the intruder is a Peregrine or Golden Eagle, pandemonium will ensue.

DECEMBER

Siskin

Fieldfare

Robin

Waxwing

SPECIES TICK LIST

	JAN	FEB	MAR	APR	MAY	JUN	JUL	AUG	SEP	OCT	NOV	DEC
Red-throated Diver												
Black-throated Diver												
Great Northern Diver												
Little Grebe												
Great Crested Grebe												
Red-necked Grebe												
Slavonian Grebe												
Black-necked Grebe												
Fulmar												
Manx Shearwater												
Storm Petrel												
Leach's Storm-petrel												
Gannet												
Cormorant												
Shag												
Bittern												
Little Egret												
Grey Heron												
Mute Swan												
Bewick's Swan												
Whooper Swan												
Bean Goose												
Pink-footed Goose												
White-fronted Goose												
Greylag Goose												
Canada Goose												
Barnacle Goose												
Brent Goose												
Egyptian Goose												
Shelduck												
Mandarin Duck												
Wigeon												
Gadwall												
Teal												
Mallard												
Pintail												
Garganey												
Shoveler												
Pochard												
Tufted Duck												
Scaup												
Eider												
Long-tailed Duck												
Common Scoter												
Velvet Scoter												
Goldeneye												
Smew												
Red-breasted Merganser												
Goosander												
Ruddy Duck												
Osprey												
Honey Buzzard												
Red Kite												
Marsh Harrier												
Hen Harrier												
Montagu's Harrier												
Goshawk												
Sparrowhawk												
Buzzard												
Golden Eagle												

	JAN	FEB	MAR	APR	MAY	JUN	JUL	AUG	SEP	OCT	NOV	DEC
Kestrel												
Merlin												
Hobby												
Peregrine												
Red Grouse												
Ptarmigan												
Black Grouse												
Capercaillie												
Red-legged Partridge												
Grey Partridge												
Quail												
Pheasant												
Spotted Crake												
Water Rail												
Corncrake												
Moorhen												
Coot												
Oystercatcher												
Avocet												
Stone Curlew												
Little Ringed Plover												
Ringed Plover												
Dotterel												
Golden Plover												
Grey Plover												
Lapwing												
Knot												
Sanderling												
Little Stint												
Temminck's Stint												
Curlew Sandpiper												
Purple Sandpiper												
Dunlin												
Ruff												
Jack Snipe												
Snipe												
Woodcock												
Black-tailed Godwit												
Bar-tailed Godwit												
Whimbrel												
Curlew												
Spotted Redshank												
Redshank												
Greenshank												
Green Sandpiper												
Wood Sandpiper												
Common Sandpiper												
Turnstone												
Red-necked Phalarope												
Pomarine Skua												
Arctic Skua												
Great Skua												
Mediterranean Gull												
Little Gull												
Black-headed Gull												
Common Gull												
Lesser Black-backed Gull												
Yellow-legged Gull												
Herring Gull												
Iceland Gull												

SPECIES TICK LIST

	JAN	FEB	MAR	APR	MAY	JUN	JUL	AUG	SEP	OCT	NOV	DEC
Glaucous Gull												
Great Black-backed Gull												
Kittiwake												
Sandwich Tern												
Roseate Tern												
Common Tern												
Arctic Tern												
Little Tern												
Black Tern												
Guillemot												
Razorbill												
Black Guillemot												
Little Auk												
Puffin												
Feral Pigeon/Rock Dove												
Stock Dove												
Woodpigeon												
Collared Dove												
Turtle Dove												
Ring-necked Parakeet												
Cuckoo												
Barn Owl												
Little Owl												
Tawny Owl												
Long-eared Owl												
Short-eared Owl												
Nightjar												
Swift												
Kingfisher												
Wryneck												
Green Woodpecker												
Great Spotted Woodpecker												
Lesser Spotted Woodpecker												
Woodlark												
Skylark												
Shore Lark												
Sand Martin												
Swallow												
House Martin												
Tree Pipit												
Meadow Pipit												
Rock Pipit												
Water Pipit												
Yellow Wagtail												
Grey Wagtail												
Pied Wagtail												
Waxwing												
Dipper												
Wren												
Dunnock												
Robin												
Nightingale												
Black Redstart												
Redstart												
Whinchat												
Stonechat												
Wheatear												
Ring Ouzel												
Blackbird												
Fieldfare												

	JAN	FEB	MAR	APR	MAY	JUN	JUL	AUG	SEP	OCT	NOV	DEC
Song Thrush												
Redwing												
Mistle Thrush												
Cetti's Warbler												
Grasshopper Warbler												
Sedge Warbler												
Marsh Warbler												
Reed Warbler												
Dartford Warbler												
Lesser Whitethroat												
Common Whitethroat												
Garden Warbler												
Blackcap												
Wood Warbler												
Chiffchaff												
Willow Warbler												
Goldcrest												
Firecrest												
Spotted Flycatcher												
Pied Flycatcher												
Bearded Tit												
Long-tailed Tit												
Marsh Tit												
Willow Tit												
Crested Tit												
Coal Tit												
Blue Tit												
Great Tit												
Nuthatch												
Treecreeper												
Red-backed Shrike												
Great Grey Shrike												
Jay												
Magpie												
Chough												
Jackdaw												
Rook												
Carrion Crow/Hooded Crow												
Raven												
Starling												
House Sparrow												
Tree Sparrow												
Chaffinch												
Brambling												
Greenfinch												
Goldfinch												
Siskin												
Linnet												
Twite												
Redpoll												
Common Crossbill												
Scottish Crossbill												
Bullfinch												
Hawfinch												
Lapland Bunting												
Snow Bunting												
Yellowhammer												
Cirl Bunting												
Reed Bunting												
Corn Bunting												

ILLUSTRATED CHECK LIST OF THE BIRDS OF BRITAIN AND IRELAND

This check list, presented in taxonomic order, is designed to help you identify the most common species found in Britain and Ireland along with your own notes and sketches. Each entry gives the species scientific name, size and most frequented habitats.

KEY

 Coastal includes estuaries

 Farmland includes farmland and grassland

 Heathland

 Upland includes mountains and moorlands

 Urban includes urban and built-up areas

Wetland includes rivers, lakes, reservoirs and marshes

Woodland includes parks and gardens

(**BP**) **Breeding Plumage**

(**NB**) **Non-breeding Plumage**

♂ **Male**   ♀ **Female**

Red-throated Diver
Gavia stellata   52-58cm

  (**BP**)

Black-throated Diver
Gavia arctica   58-68cm

  (**BP**)

Great Northern Diver
Gavia immer   68-81cm

(**BP**)

Little Grebe
Tachybaptus ruficollis   27cm

(**BP**)

Great Crested Grebe
Podiceps cristatus   48cm

  (**BP**)

Red-necked Grebe
Podiceps grisegena   33cm

  (**BP**)

Slavonian Grebe
Podiceps auritus   33cm

  (**NB**)

Black-necked Grebe
Podiceps nigricapillus   30cm

  (**NB**)

Fulmar
Fulmarus glacialis   47cm

Manx Shearwater
Puffinus puffinus   35cm

Storm Petrel
Hydrobates pelagicus   15cm

Leach's Storm-petrel
Oceanodroma leucorrhoa   20cm

Gannet
Morus bassanus   90cm

Cormorant
Phalacrocorax carbo   90cm

    (**BP**)

Shag
Phalacrocorax aristotelis   76cm

Bittern
Botaurus stellaris   75cm

Little Egret
Egretta garzetta   60cm

Grey Heron
Ardea cinerea   90cm

Mute Swan
Cygnus olor   152cm

Bewick's Swan
Cygnus columbianus   122cm

Whooper Swan
Cygnus cygnus   152cm

Bean Goose
Anser fabalis   66-84cm

Pink-footed Goose
Anser brachyrhyncus   68cm

White-fronted Goose
Anser albifrons   66-76cm

Greylag Goose
Anser anser   76-89cm

Canada Goose
Branta canadensis   97cm

Barnacle Goose
Branta leucopsis   58-69cm

Brent Goose
Branta bernicla   56-61cm

Egyptian Goose
Alopochen aegyptiacus   68cm

Shelduck
Tadorna tadorna   61cm   ♂

Mandarin Duck
Aix galericulata   43cm   ♂

Wigeon
Anas penelope   45cm   ♂

Gadwall
Anas strepera   51cm   ♂

Teal
Anas crecca   51cm   ♂

Mallard
Anas platyrhynchos 58cm
♂

Pintail
Anas acuta 58cm
♂

Garganey
Anas querquedula 38cm
♂

Shoveler
Anas clypeata 51cm
♂

Pochard
Aythya ferina 46cm ♂

Tufted Duck
Aythya fuligula 44cm ♂

Scaup
Aythya marila 46cm ♂

Eider
Somateria mollissima 61cm
♂

Long-tailed Duck
Clangula hyemalis 36-46cm
NB ♂

Common Scoter
Melanitta nigra 48cm ♂

Velvet Scoter
Melanitta fusca 56cm ♂

Goldeneye
Bucephala clangula 45cm
♂

Smew
Mergus albellus 38cm ♂

Red-breasted Merganser
Mergus serrator 52-58cm
♂

Goosander
Mergus merganser 58-66cm
♂

Ruddy Duck
Oxyura jamaicensis 40cm
♂

Osprey
Pandion haliaetus 55-69cm

Honey Buzzard
Pernis apivorus 50-58cm

Red Kite
Milvus milvus 60-70cm

Marsh Harrier
Circus aeruginosus 48-56cm ♂

Hen Harrier
Circus cyaneus 48-50cm ♂

Montagu's Harrier
Circus pygargus 43-47cm
 ♂

Goshawk
Accipiter gentilis 48-60cm
 ♂

Sparrowhawk
Accipiter nisus 30-41cm
    ♂

Buzzard
Buteo buteo 43-53cm

Golden Eagle
Aquila chrysaetos 75-86cm

Kestrel
Falco tinnunculus 33-39cm
   ♂

Merlin
Falco columbarius 25-30cm
   ♂

Hobby
Falco subbuteo 28-35cm

Peregrine
Falco peregrinus 39-50cm

Red Grouse
Lagopus lagopus 38cm ♂

Ptarmigan
Lagopus mutus 35cm
 ♂

Black Grouse
Tetrao tetrix 40-55cm ♂

Capercaillie
Tetrao urogallus 60-87cm ♂

Red-legged Partridge
Alectoris rufa 33cm

Grey Partridge
Perdix perdix 30cm

Quail
Coturnix coturnix 18cm ♂

Pheasant
Phasianus colchicus 55-85cm
 ♂

Spotted Crake
Porzana porzana 23cm

Water Rail
Rallus aquaticus 25cm

Corncrake
Crex crex 26cm

Moorhen
Gallinula chloropus 33cm

Coot
Fulica atra 38cm

Oystercatcher
Haematopus ostralegus 43cm

Avocet
Recurvirostra avosetta 41cm

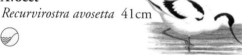

Stone Curlew
Burhinus oedicnemus 43cm

Little Ringed Plover
Charadrius dubius 15cm

Ringed Plover
Charadrius hiaticula 17cm

Dotterel
Charadrius morinellus 21cm

Golden Plover
Pluvialis apricaria 27cm

Grey Plover
Pluvialis squatarola 30cm

Lapwing
Vanellus vanellus 30cm

Knot
Calidris canutus 25cm

Sanderling
Calidris alba 20cm

Little Stint
Calidris minuta 13cm

Temminck's Stint
Calidris temminckii 13cm

Juvenile

Curlew Sandpiper
Calidris ferruginea 20cm

Juvenile

Purple Sandpiper
Calidris maritima 21cm

Dunlin
Calidris alpina 18cm

Ruff
Philomachus pugnax 20-30cm

Jack Snipe
Lymnocryptes minimus 19cm

Snipe
Gallinago gallinago 26cm

Woodcock
Scolopax rusticola 34cm

Black-tailed Godwit
Limosa limosa 38-44cm

Bar-tailed Godwit
Limosa lapponica 36-40cm

Whimbrel
Numenius phaeopus 40cm

Curlew
Numenius arquata 50-60cm

Spotted Redshank
Tringa erythropus 30cm

Redshank
Tringa totanus 26cm

Greenshank
Tringa nebularia 30cm

Green Sandpiper
Tringa ochropus 23cm

Wood Sandpiper
Tringa glareola 20cm

Common Sandpiper
Actitis hypoleucos 20cm

Turnstone
Arenaria interpres 22cm

Red-necked Phalarope
Phalaropus lobatus 18cm

Pomarine Skua
Stercorarius pomarinus 46-50cm

Arctic Skua
Stercorarius parasiticus 41-45cm

Great Skua
Stercorarius skua 58cm

Mediterranean Gull
Larus melanocephalus 38cm

Little Gull
Larus minutus 26cm
 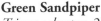

Black-headed Gull
Larus ridibundus 36cm

    **BP**

Common Gull
Larus canus 40-43cm

    BP

Lesser Black-backed Gull
Larus fuscus 52-62cm

   **BP**

Yellow-legged Gull
Larus cachinnans 58-68cm

  BP

Herring Gull
Larus argentatus 53-66cm

 BP

Iceland Gull
Larus glaucoides 52-63cm

 BP

Glaucous Gull
Larus hyperboreus 62-72cm

 BP

Great Black-backed Gull
Larus marinus 65-75cm

Kittiwake
Rissa tridactyla 40cm

 BP

Sandwich Tern
Sterna sandvicensis 40cm

 BP

Roseate Tern
Sterna dougallii 36cm

 BP

Common Tern
Sterna hirundo 34cm

  BP

Arctic Tern
Sterna paradisaea 34cm

 BP

Little Tern
Sterna albifrons 23cm

 BP

Black Tern
Chlidonias niger 23cm

  BP

Guillemot
Uria aalge 40cm

 BP

Razorbill
Alca torda 38cm

 BP

Black Guillemot
Cepphus grylle 30-32cm

 BP

Little Auk
Alle alle 19cm

 NB

Puffin
Fratercula arctica 28cm

 BP

Feral Pigeon/Rock Dove
Columba livia 33cm

Stock Dove
Columba oenas 33cm

Woodpigeon
Columba palumbus 41cm

Collared Dove
Streptopelia decaocto 32cm

Turtle Dove
Streptopelia turtur 26cm

Ring-necked Parakeet
Psittacula krameri 38-42cm

Cuckoo
Cuculus canorus 33cm

Barn Owl
Tyto alba 33-39cm

Little Owl
Athene noctua 21-23cm

Tawny Owl
Strix aluco 38cm

Long-eared Owl
Asio otus 35-37cm

Short-eared Owl
Asio flammeus 34-42cm

Nightjar
Caprimulgus europaeus 27cm

Swift
Apus apus 16-17cm

Kingfisher
Alcedo atthis 16-17cm

Wryneck
Jynx torquilla 16-17cm

Green Woodpecker ♂
Picus viridis 31-33cm

Great Spotted Woodpecker ♂
Dendrocopos major 22-23cm

Lesser Spotted Woodpecker ♂
Dendrocopos minor 15cm

Woodlark
Lullula arborea 15cm

Skylark
Alauda arvensis 18-19cm

Shore Lark
Eremophila alpestris 16-17cm

Sand Martin
Riparia riparia 12cm

Swallow
Hirundo rustica 17-19cm

House Martin
Delichon urbica 12.5cm

Tree Pipit
Anthus trivialis 15cm

Meadow Pipit
Anthus pratensis 14.5cm

Rock Pipit
Anthus petrosus 16.5cm

Water Pipit
Anthus spinoletta 16.5cm

Yellow Wagtail
Motacilla flava 17cm

Grey Wagtail
Motacilla cinerea 18-20cm

♂

Pied Wagtail
Motacilla alba 18cm

♂

Waxwing
Bombycilla garrulus 18cm

Dipper
Cinclus cinclus 18cm

Wren
Troglodytes troglodytes 9-10cm

Dunnock
Prunella modularis 14.5cm

Robin
Erithacus rubecula 14cm

Nightingale
Luscinia megarhynchos 16.5cm

Black Redstart
Phoenicurus ochruros 14.5cm

♂

Redstart
Phoenicurus phoenicurus 14cm

♂

Whinchat
Saxicola rubetra 12-13cm ♂

Stonechat
Saxicola torquata 12.5cm ♂

Wheatear
Oenanthe oenanthe 15-16cm
 ♂

Ring Ouzel
Turdus torquatus 24cm ♂

Blackbird
Turdus merula 24-25cm ♂

Fieldfare
Turdus pilaris 25cm

Song Thrush
Turdus philomelos 23cm

Redwing
Turdus iliacus 21cm

Mistle Thrush
Turdus viscivorus 27cm

Cetti's Warbler
Cettia cetti 14cm

Grasshopper Warbler
Locustella naevia 13cm

Sedge Warbler
Acrocephalus schoenobaenus 13cm

Marsh Warbler
Acrocephalus palustris 13cm

Reed Warbler
Acrocephalus scirpaceus 13cm

Dartford Warbler
Sylvia undata 13cm
 ♂

Lesser Whitethroat
Sylvia curruca 13.5cm

Common Whitethroat
Sylvia communis 14cm ♂

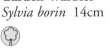

Garden Warbler
Sylvia borin 14cm

Blackcap
Sylvia atricapilla 14cm ♂

Wood Warbler
Phylloscopus sibilatrix 12.5cm

Chiffchaff
Phylloscopus collybita 10-11cm

Willow Warbler
Phylloscopus trochilus 11cm

Goldcrest
Regulus regulus 9cm

♀

Firecrest
Regulus ignicapillus 9cm

♀
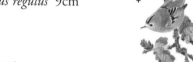

Spotted Flycatcher
Muscicapa striata 14cm

Pied Flycatcher
Ficedula hypoleuca 13cm ♂

Bearded Tit
Panurus biarmicus 16.5cm

♂

♀

Long-tailed Tit
Aegithalos caudatus 14cm

Marsh Tit
Parus palustris 11.5cm

Willow Tit
Parus montanus 11.5cm

Crested Tit
Parus cristatus 11.5cm

Coal Tit
Parus ater 11.5cm

Blue Tit
Parus caeruleus 12cm

Great Tit
Parus major 14cm

Nuthatch
Sitta europaea 14cm

Treecreeper
Certhia familiaris 12.5cm

Red-backed Shrike
Lanius collurio 17cm

♂

Great Grey Shrike
Lanius excubitor 25cm

Jay
Garrulus glandarius 34cm

Magpie
Pica pica 46cm

Chough
Pyrrhocorax pyrrhocorax 40cm

Jackdaw
Corvus monedula 33-34cm

Rook
Corvus frugilegus 44-46cm

Carrion Crow/Hooded Crow
Corvus corone 47cm

Raven
Corvus corax 65cm

Starling
Sturnus vulgaris 21cm

House Sparrow
Passer domesticus 15cm ♂

Tree Sparrow
Passer montanus 14cm

Chaffinch
Fringilla coelebs 15cm ♂

Brambling
Fringilla montifringilla 15cm

Greenfinch
Carduelis chloris 15cm ♂

Goldfinch
Carduelis carduelis 12cm

Siskin
Carduelis spinus 12cm ♂

Linnet
Carduelis cannabina 14cm ♂

Twite
Carduelis flavirostris 14cm

Redpoll
Carduelis flammea 12-13cm ♂

Common Crossbill
Loxia curvirostra 16.5cm ♂

Scottish Crossbill
Loxia scotica 16.5cm ♂

Bullfinch
Pyrrhula pyrrhula 15cm ♂

Hawfinch
Coccothraustes coccothraustes 18cm

 ♂

Lapland Bunting
Calcarius lapponicus 15.5cm

♀
♂

Cirl Bunting
Emberiza cirlus 16.5cm
♀

♂

Snow Bunting ♂
Plectrophenax nivalis 16-17cm

Reed Bunting
Emberiza schoeniclus 15.5cm
♂

Yellowhammer
Emberiza citrinella 16.5cm

♂

Corn Bunting
Miliaria calandra 18cm

RECOMMENDED READING

Attracting Birds to Your Garden
Cottridge, Moss
(New Holland, 1998)

Bill Oddie's Birding Map of Britain and Ireland
(New Holland, 2001)

Bill Oddie's Birds of Britain and Ireland
(New Holland, 1998)

Birds of Britain and Ireland
Couzens (HarperCollins, 1997)

The Birdwatcher's Yearbook and Diary
Buckingham Press, 55 Thorpe Park Road,
Peterborough, Cambridgeshire PE3 6LJ.
Published annually.

Collins Field Guide to the Birds of Britain and Europe
Mullarney, Svensson, Zetterstrom, Grant
(HarperCollins, 1999)

Collins Top British Birding Spots: The 130 Best Places to Go Bird Watching
Tipling (HarperCollins, 1999)

How to Birdwatch
Moss (New Holland, 2003)

'Where to Watch Birds in…' A series published by Helm covering all parts of the United Kingdom.

MAGAZINES

Birdwatch, available from newsagents monthly, or by subscription from *Birdwatch* (Subs Dept.), Fulham House, Goldsworth Road, Woking, Surrey GU21 1LY
Tel: 01778 392027

Birdwatching, available from newsagents monthly, or from Birdwatching subscriptions, Tower House, Sovereign Park, Market Harborough, Leicestershire LE16 9EF

CASSETTES

Teach Yourself Bird Sounds,
Couzens & Wyatt (Waxwing 1992-98)
A set of 10 cassettes, divided by habitat).

USEFUL ADDRESSES

The British Trust for Ornithology
The Nunnery, Thetford, Norfolk IP24 2PU
Tel: 01842 750050   www.bto.org

Royal Society for the Protection of Birds
The Lodge, Sandy, Bedfordshire SG19 2DL
Tel: 01767 680551   www.rspb.org.uk

Scottish Ornithologists' Club
Harbour Point, Newhailes Road
Musselburgh EH21 6SJ
Tel: 0131 653 0653   www.the-soc.org.uk

Welsh Ornithological Society
196 Chester Road, Hartford, Northwich
Cheshire CW8 1LG
Tel: 01606 77960
www.members.aol.com/welshos/cac

The Wildfowl & Wetlands Trust
Slimbridge, Gloucestershire GL2 7BT
Tel: 01453 890333   www.wwt.org.uk

The Wildlife Trusts
The Kiln, Waterside, Mather Road
Newark, Nottinghamshire NG24 1WT
Tel: 0870 0367711   www.wildlifetrusts.org

OPTICAL DEALERS

In Focus
(Branches in Gloucestershire,
Hertfordshire, Lancashire, London,
Norfolk, Rutland, West Sussex, Yorkshire)
www.at-infocus.co.uk

London Camera Exchange
98 The Strand, London WC2R 0AG
Tel: 020 7379 0200   www.lcegroup.co.uk

WEBSITES

www.birdcare.com/birdon/
www.birdguides.com
www.birdwords.co.uk
www.fatbirder.com

Tree Sparrows

INDEX